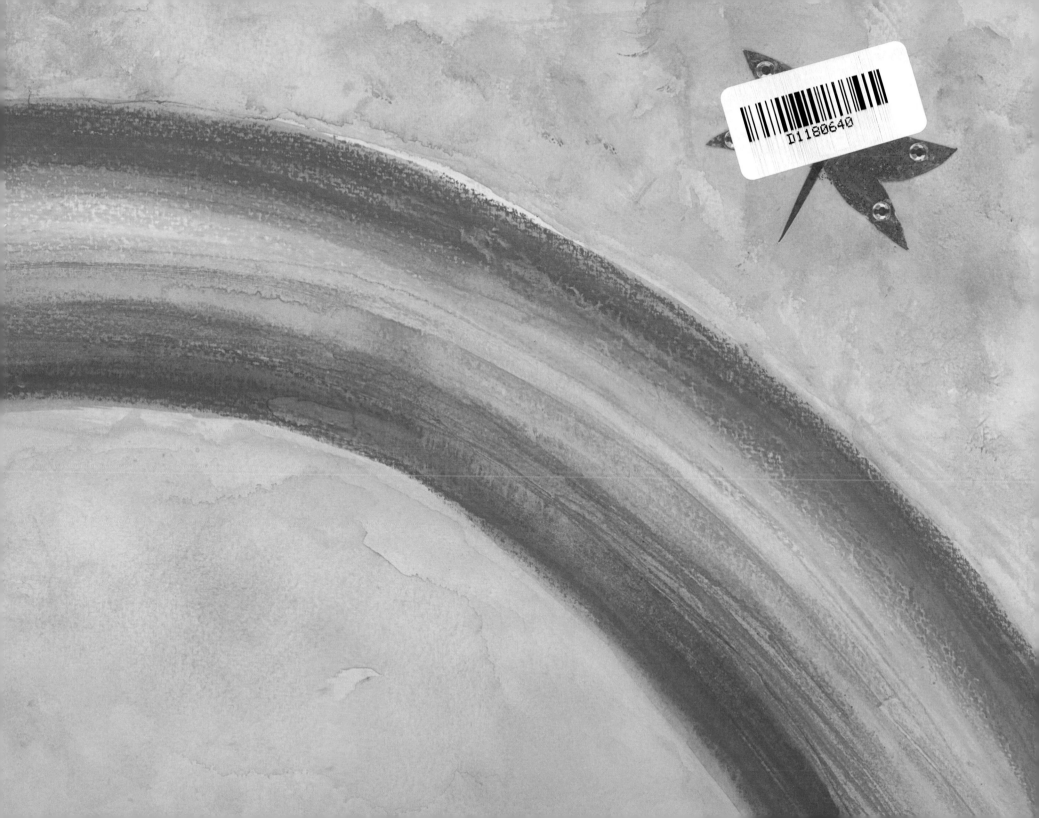

With wings of
LOVE,
WENdi KNOX

fromMuckto Magic

an uplifting journey

written, illustrated and lived

by **Wendi Knox**

ISBN 978-0-692-16922-3

Published in the United States

Immaginare Press

Los Angeles

Written and Illustrated by Wendi Knox

Immaginare Press

immaginarepress.com

printed in China

Dragonflies spend most of their lives stuck in the muck at the bottom of a pond. While crawling down there, they grow their magical wings. I hope this book helps you grow yours.

XoWendi

This book was born in the muck of my own self-doubt. It's for all of us who struggle to rise up from the darkness of self-diminishment to the light of self-love.

These words and paintings came to me on the wings of dragonflies. Now, it's my honor to pay their magic forward to you.

Have you ever been stuck, so stuck in the muck

With the yuck and the guck, that you thought "What the !*#?"

You're crawling down there

Through the fears and the tears

The Shoulda's, The Woulda's

And How'd-I-Get-Here's

Through the slime of self-doubt and the dreariest dread

All those nasty old voices that yak in your head

But what if instead…

you accepted the muck

And were sweet to yourself

Now that wouldn't suck

You could nurture in nature and lull in the bath

And give yourself flowers

A good cry or a laugh

Just let yourself breathe, now that would be new

And set yourself free

To feel red, green or blue

Because being stuck in the muck and the yuck isn't tragic

It's just how we dragonflies

grow our own magic.

The story behind this storybook.

Once upon a time, I had a big office, a big salary and a really big job. I was the only female Senior Vice-President/Creative Director at one of the biggest advertising agencies in Los Angeles.

It was the kind of job I dreamed about in my twenties. But in my forties, it felt like a prison sentence. I was silenced and negated. And my voice was screaming to get out.

Unexpectedly, I got my chance. At 50, I lost my big fat advertising job. And found myself stuck in the muck of fear, worry and reinvention.

One day, sobbing in my backyard, I begged the universe, "Am I too old to reinvent myself? Please give me a sign."

Well, I got a sign alright. I went for a walk and came home to find my entire backyard filled with red dragonflies. Seriously. Hundreds of red dragonflies, whirling and twirling above me for hours.

I learned that dragonflies spend most of their lives stuck in the muck, crawling around the bottom of a pond—for up to four years, in fact.

Then, one seemingly random day, the dragonfly climbs up onto a reed or leaf into the sunlight. And there, her wings magically unfurl. It turns out they'd been growing all that time.

That's when I got it. I'M A DRAGONFLY. And my wings were growing the whole time I was stuck in my muck.

Well, after that miraculous event, I started seeing dragonflies everywhere. On freeways. At shopping centers. You name it. And they were there.

I know this sounds crazy, but I believe those dragonflies were recruiting me to share this story with the world. So now, that's exactly what I'm doing.

I hope their story inspires yours.

xo Wendi

Here's some magic

that grew out of my muck...

What magic will grow out of *your* muck?

About the author/artist/uplifter.

Wendi Knox is on a mission to uplift and inspire women to transform their muck into magic.

She's sharing her art, her heart and The Way Of The Dragonfly, encouraging others to rise up and spread their wings.

Wendi is grateful for her husband Will, son Landon, fur-baby Blossom and for the magic of living in Ojai, California.

For more inspiration, fly over to WendiKnox.com